A robber at Pop's

Written by Bronwyn Tainui
Illustrated by Fabiano Fiorin

Nick and Pop are shooting a film with a robber in it today.

What are they doing?

Pop is the robber. He has all the right gear for a robber. He has a sack he will fill with loot.

Ruff will be in the film. Can we dress Ruff up? He can put on robber's gear, too.

Ruff is all right as he is. Dogs do not need to dress up.

Pop rushes to the ladder.

Keep going, Pop! Go up that ladder!

What is Pop doing now?

Pop is going up the ladder.

Good, Pop! Quick as you can! Keep on going right up to the top.

Pop is too old to be doing that!

Pop comes back down the ladder.

We are shooting a film. I am a robber in it.

That's right. Pop is just dressed up.

Nick is still filming.

You can film the car, but do not film me.

All right.

Pop gets his card out of his pocket.

Pop

PC Colin looks at Pop's card.

That is proof that I am me.

Will Pop go to jail?

Ruff barks at Frank and Flora.

Do not panic. There are no robbers here.

Not with me here!

Woof!

You must tell us when you next shoot a film, Pop!

Woof! Woof!

The car is off. Nick starts filming it.

PC Colin said filming his car was all right.

Woof! Woof!

Pop points here and there.

Right, Frank, you stand there. Flora, you run at me with that broom.

Me?

Pop has packed his sack with loot. The sack is full.

You missed this bit.

Nick films Pop creeping off with his full sack.

Pop looks just like a robber, now.

Pop runs off. But Flora is quick. She bumps Pop with the broom.

Oh no! What is Flora up to?

Pop slips into some pots.

Keep filming, Nick! Keep shooting!

This will be a top film.

Oops, I think Flora pushed Pop too hard!

Flora is off, too!

"Rotten robber! Get going! Do not come back or I will get you with this broom!"

Pop runs.

"Help!"

Wow, see Pop go! He is not looking old now.

Soon, they are all puffed.

"Huff, puff!"

"Cut! We have a film!"

"Thank goodness."

They all clap. Nick grins.

"I cannot wait to see this film."

"It will be a good one. Flora is a star."